A GUIDE FOR AN EXCELLENT OVERVIEW BUSINESS

.

MARION R SWANSON

TABLE OF CONTENTS

INTRODUCTION

SECTION ONE

SECTION TWO

SECTION SEVEN

Cultural Quirks And How They Affect Marketing

Cultural Aspects and How They Affect the Memorability of the Ad

Social Media's Function In International Product Launches

SECTION EIGHT

Digital Transformation's Effect On Company Sales

How Can You Go Beyond The Obstacles In Branding?

SECTION NINE

Impact Of Sale: Direct Versus Indirect Methods Of Distribution

Benefits Of Direct Distribution Routes

INTRODUCTION

Many prosperous companies make enough money for their owners—who could be investors or shareholders, depending on the kind of company—to expand and lead secure lives. Nevertheless, some small business owners are prepared to forgo some earnings in order to provide a service with a social mission, produce an eco-friendly product, or maintain a better work-life balance. Every entrepreneur defines success in their firm in a somewhat different way. You answered "YES" to the urge to launch your own company and made the audacious decision to bring your aspirations to life as a fearless business owner. Excellent work. You may be starting a new business, or you may already have one that is ready to grow and scale. You know that time is valuable and that, in addition to managing work, life, and everything in between, you want to make the most of it by dedicating your efforts to expanding and building your company. Furthermore, you have now reached a crucial, difficult turning point in your growth plans as you consider strengthening your relationship with your clients and developing strategies to develop, scale, and greatly increase your company. A few of the inquiries you might have to consider Success in business can take many various forms for different organizations. Sales indicators are important to some, but social effect is important to others. Creating sustainable growth and development and long-term profitability are more important to a successful firm than making quick money. A successful business can be defined in a variety of ways, but common characteristics include growth, profitability, and customer happiness. A business that can turn a profit while continuing to develop and expand is generally considered successful. Furthermore, a flourishing enterprise Is often one that can fulfill the requirements and anticipations of its clientele.

SECTION ONE

THE Type And Ambit Of A Profitable Company

A well-defined and purposeful goal and vision are essential components of a successful organization. This entails knowing what makes the company special and useful to its clients and having a clear aim or purpose for the enterprise. A successful business's size and reach are referred to as its scope. Even though a successful firm may begin small, it may eventually grow into a huge organization with a global presence. Let's begin by discussing the goals and objectives of a prosperous company. The mission statement encapsulates the purpose and motivation of the firm, serving as its "why" as well as its goals. The exact aims and objectives that the company is pursuing make up the "what" of the firm, or the vision. For instance, a prosperous restaurant's goal could be to serve its patrons tasty meals at a reasonable price. Maybe the goal is to become the city's most well-liked restaurant. Elements that promote the development of businesses People that are passionate, diligent, and knowledgeable in their fields of specialty are essential to any successful organization. These workers ought to be dedicated to assisting the company in its success and in line with its goals and mission. They should also be able to function successfully as a team and be receptive to criticism and new information. Possessing a distinctive good or service that addresses a genuine need or issue is another essential component of a successful business. A prosperous company might, for instance, provide a novel kind of software that facilitates employees' work. Alternatively, it might provide a novel food variety that is more hygienic or practical than what's already offered. Offering something that is genuinely superior to what is currently available on the market is crucial. Numerous variables might promote the expansion and prosperity of a corporation.

Elements That Support The Development Of A Business Into A Profitable Enterprise

Among the most crucial elements are:

- A capable and committed workforce. - An original good or service that addresses a pressing issue or fills a gap in the market.

- A strong marketing plan that targets the appropriate demographic.

- An emphasis on delivering top-notch customer service and ensuring client happiness.

- A readiness to modify and adjust to the market. Elements that promote company success or failure There are several important causes of business failure.

A typical explanation is that there isn't enough consumer demand for the good or service the company is providing. The company won't be able to make enough money to pay its expenses and turn a profit if there isn't enough demand for the goods or services. A further factor contributing to business failure is subpar management choices. For instance, poor hiring, pricing, or marketing decisions may cause the company to experience financial difficulties. Insufficient cash flow is yet another frequent cause of company collapse.

A business may fail even if it is successful if it does not have enough cash on hand to pay its bills. This may occur if the company is expanding too quickly or if client payments are not being collected on time. Lack of money is another factor that could contribute to a business's demise. A company might not be able to compete in its field if it lacks the funds to spend in expansion.

Let's concentrate on a single cause of company failure

inadequate market research: This can occur when a company enters a new market without conducting adequate research to understand its target audience. For instance, a company may create a new product that isn't tailored to its target market, or it may set its prices too high or too low.

In either scenario, drawing clients and turning a profit will be challenging for the company. One more instance. Assume a company has conducted market research and has a solid understanding of both its target market and its consumer base. But the company underestimates the competition, which is a mistake. It may believe that it will be the only company providing a particular good or service, but in actuality, there are several companies providing the same thing. This may result in fierce competition, which could make it challenging for the company to turn a profit.

SECTION TWO

What Is The Nature Of Entrepreneurship and How Important Is It?

Apart from the traits and incentives of entrepreneurs, the essence of entrepreneurship includes its significance in the economy. There are various reasons why entrepreneurship is significant:

- It stimulates economic growth by establishing new companies and sectors of the economy.

- It gives people opportunity and work. It raises living standards and stimulates innovation. - It promotes efficiency and competition in the economy.

- It may result in the development of wealth and a more fair allocation of resources. It can raise standards of living and encourage social transformation. Because of all these advantages, entrepreneurship is essential to any economy.

The significance of entrepreneurship A part of being an entrepreneur is looking for new opportunities.It brings about new endeavors, occupations, and tasks for society. It develops fresh economic principles.It generates capital and riches for the nation.

Reasons For The Significance Of Entrepreneurship

The importance of entrepreneurship to the economy and society at large is multifaceted.

One explanation is that creativity and innovation are fostered by entrepreneurship. Entrepreneurs are frequently willing to try new things and take chances, which can result in the creation of new goods and services. Consequently, this can promote economic expansion and employment creation.

The fact that entrepreneurship fosters competition is another factor. In a competitive market, companies must put in great effort to set themselves apart from the competition and provide the greatest goods and services. Customers gain from this since they have more options and better deals. The potential for entrepreneurship to bring about social and cultural transformation is another factor in its significance.

To improve the world, for instance, is a common goal shared by many business owners. They may design goods or services that make people's lives better, or they could utilize their companies to promote social issues. Thus, entrepreneurship has the potential to benefit society at large. And last, becoming an entrepreneur offers chances for development on a personal level. Entrepreneurs frequently grow their networks, pick up new abilities, and acquire new experiences.

1 missions that spur entrepreneurs to start their own businesses Capacity to meet your financial needs: A lot of entrepreneurs, like myself, launch their businesses with the express intent of becoming extremely wealthy. You would be gravely erroneous to believe that the business founder's financial success is a given. Research indicates that there is a greater likelihood of becoming affluent if you work in a stable firm at a high level. If you are aware of this, money will probably not be a

major factor in your first motivations or in your chances of making significant money early in the lifecycle of your firm.

2. Motivation from the mission: Do your company's objectives go beyond individual fulfillment? I refer to this as your mission. Some believe that a mission must tackle world-changing issues. Others see it as something much simpler, such as having a positive influence on your immediate surroundings (family, neighborhood, coworkers, etc.). An idea might occasionally act as the cornerstone of your startup. On occasion, the mission statement is developed later on in the company's development or during a shift to new offerings and business strategies. You can have any kind of objective as long as it is real, something that inspires you to rise to the challenges of each day and gets you out of bed in the morning.

3. Monetary gains: Making money is the ultimate goal of any company endeavor, traditional or entrepreneurial. Entrepreneurs want the highest possible financial rewards, but they also experience greater fulfillment in the process. First of all, they are self-employed, which is a powerful incentive in and of itself. Second, they think that in addition to

producing money, they are providing the industry with cutting-edge business solutions.

4. Entrepreneurs are motivated and aided in reaching their objectives by creative control. Every artistic choice has to be in line with the entrepreneurs' mission. For example, a product is introduced with the intention of reaching a younger audience. Every creative choice, from product design to marketing tactics, must be made in order to appeal to a specific base.

5. Greater freedom: Compared to traditional systems, entrepreneurial ones offer greater freedom. More flexibility in the working structure is what entrepreneurs desire. They are more free to decide what they believe will be best for the business in the long run.

The Purpose And Goals Of Being An Entrepreneur

1. Following interests: The motivation behind starting an entrepreneurial endeavor is the desire of the founders to pursue their interests. They are motivated to implement their creative business solutions because they firmly believe in them.

2. Identifying market gaps: Finding market gaps is one of the main goals of entrepreneurial endeavors. Entrepreneurs profit from the requirement for a distinctive business solution.

3. Own boss: One of the main motivations for being an entrepreneur is the fact that they are their own bosses. They aspire to take the initiative and make crucial choices for the business.

4. Another important consideration here is flexible work times. The core principles of entrepreneurship are self-accountability and employee empowerment.

5. Money: Earning much more money is not possible in traditional employment responsibilities. Entrepreneurs aim to offer company ideas that will boost their own purchasing power.

What Does Small And Large Firms' Marketing Management Entail?

First, let us discuss tiny firms. One of the most crucial marketing tactics for small businesses is to have a distinctive brand identity that sets them apart from the competitors.

- Building a robust social media presence in order to engage with clients.

– Establishing a favorable internet and word-of-mouth reputation.

- Providing rewards and loyalty schemes to attract and keep clients. Establishing alliances with neighborhood small companies.

These are just a few of the methods small companies can employ to effectively sell their goods and services.

SECTION THREE

Methods For Launching A Business

Conducting market research is a crucial step in launching a new company. This entails researching the market to comprehend the demands of prospective clients as well as the competitive environment. Among the specialized methods used in market research are focus groups and surveys.

- Secondary research, which includes reading studies and reports from the industry. Examining information gleaned via search engines and social media.

- Conducting interviews with sector experts. Entrepreneurs can better understand their target market and create goods and services that cater to their demands by conducting market research. Creating a business plan is a crucial step in launching a new venture.

A business plan is a written document that describes the objectives and plans of the company. It ought to contain the following:

- The vision and mission of the company. -- A market and competitor analysis. An explanation of the good or service. - An advertising strategy.

- A budget. A schedule for accomplishing the company's objectives. An effective business plan can assist entrepreneurs in obtaining capital and growing their company. A company plan and market research are important, but entrepreneurs also need to think about their finance sources. Financing a new business can come from a variety of sources, such as:

- Personal savings. – Bank or other financial institution loans. - The crowdfunding model.

- Funding for ventures. • Angel financiers. The needs of the particular business will determine which funding source is best. Putting together a good team is a crucial component of beginning a new business. A team of skilled and committed individuals is necessary to turn any bright idea or well-thought-out business plan into a reality. Employers who are able to support the growth of their company and who possess the necessary expertise and experience should be the first priority for entrepreneurs.

How Can Small Businesses Develop a Relationship with Their Customers?

1. Use your brand as a reference. It's critical to fulfill the promises made by your branding and marketing regarding the consumer experience and your company overall. You've broken your promise if you say you're always available to clients but they can never get past your voicemail when they try to reach you.

2. Adjust to their speed. Don't waste your time making small conversation or niceties with a customer who is obviously in a rush when they answer the phone. However, be careful not to cut off a caller who wants to talk on the phone too soon.

3. Recognise what matters to your clients. Always pay attention to what your consumers have to say

and how they say it to learn what matters to them. After that, adjust your plan to suit their requirements.

Other crucial actions for creating enduring relationships with customers are as follows:

- Be approachable and receptive. Make it simple for clients to contact you so that you can handle their issues.

- Have integrity and dependability. Keep your word and fulfill your promises.

- Be genuine and intimate. Demonstrate to your clients your concern for their requirements.

- Have integrity and be reliable. Establish a relationship based on trust by being open and honest. Act assertively and sociably. Go above and beyond to fulfill the demands of your clients.

How To Grow A Company

Although starting a business is a difficult process, there are some essential steps that every company must take. In order to determine whether there is a market for their goods or services, entrepreneurs should first conduct some market research. After that, they had to draft a business plan outlining their objectives and tactics.

After that, they ought to secure capital to start the company. Lastly, they want to design their sales and marketing plan and begin cultivating clientele. After the firm is up and going, it's critical to keep an eye on things and assess its progress to make sure it's headed in the correct direction. Aim for a specialized market. Serving a niche market or meeting a particular demand is frequently a more successful strategy than attempting to please everyone.

- Be unique and inventive. It's critical to differentiate yourself from the competition by providing something fresh and different.

- Establish a powerful internet presence. In order to reach clients and establish reputation, businesses must have a strong online presence in the age of the internet. - Be not frightened to change course.

- Create a powerful brand. A company can become more remembered and identifiable with a great brand.

- Give top attention to client service. Consumers value companies that go above and beyond to accommodate their demands.

- Make connections and cultivate ties. Developing contacts with professionals and other firms might help a business expand.

 - Have perseverance and patience. Building a successful business requires time and work; success does not appear immediately.

- Pay attention to ongoing education and development.

What Are A Small Business Enterprise's Management Responsibility?

 In a small business, management is responsible for multiple crucial tasks. Among them are:

- Planning: creating a company plan, establishing objectives, and choosing ways to reach those objectives. -

Organizing: Assembling the financial, material, and human resources of the company. - Staffing: Selecting, educating, and molding workers to fit the demands of the company.

 - Directing: Assisting staff members in achieving the objectives of the company through communication and guidance.

 - Controlling: keeping track of, assessing, and adjusting as needed to goals' progress.

There are still more managerial responsibilities that are unique to small companies. Among them are:

- Managing finances: This includes forecasting, accounting, and budgeting for the company's financial resources.

- Managing inventory: Monitoring stock levels and ensuring appropriate stocking and management.

 - Marketing: creating and putting into practice marketing plans to draw in and keep clients.

- Customer service: Delivering top-notch customer care to guarantee client loyalty and satisfaction.

SECTION FOUR

What Does An Entrepreneur Do As A Leader?

An entrepreneur's leadership responsibilities include establishing the company's direction and vision as well as inspiring and motivating staff to realize it. Entrepreneurs need to be able to make tough choices when they need to and convey their vision to others effectively. They also need to be able to assemble a group of workers who share their commitment to the goal and have the skills necessary to see it through. Lastly, entrepreneurs need to be flexible enough to adjust to changing conditions on the go. All things considered, an entrepreneur's leadership position is complex and calls for a variety of abilities.

Who Is In Charge?

A leader is someone who has the capacity to uplift and encourage others to accomplish a shared objective. There are leaders in every kind of organization, from small startups to multinational conglomerates. They are diverse in their characteristics. Among the traits of successful leaders are: -

Integrity: To win the respect of their followers, leaders need to be sincere and reliable. -

Vision: Future leaders need to be able to articulate their vision to others and have a clear vision for the future. - Inspiration: Leaders need to be able to motivate people to follow them and contribute to the shared objective. -

Emotional intelligence: Effective leaders are able to recognize, control, and understand both their own and others' feelings.

Self-awareness: Effective leaders must be conscious of their own advantages and disadvantages, as well as be open to criticism and self-improvement. - Innovation: Creative problem-solving and innovative thought processes are essential for leaders. -

Persistence: In the face of difficulties and disappointments, leaders need to be tenacious and not give up quickly. What characteristics of a successful leader - Clarity of purpose: A successful leader is able to explain to people the mission and objectives of the company. -

Decision-making ability: A strong leader can act in the face of ambiguity and make tough choices when called upon. - Adaptability: A capable leader is able to seize new opportunities and adjust to shifting conditions. - Integrity: Honesty and a strong sense of ethics are essential qualities for a leader. -

Empathy: A good leader must be able to relate to and comprehend the thoughts, emotions, and experiences of others.

Resilience: A successful leader must possess the capacity to endure hardships and disappointments. -

Humility: A successful leader must be able to accept responsibility for their actions, learn from them, and be receptive to criticism and fresh perspectives. Humility is a crucial trait of a successful leader. A modest leader understands that they are not an expert in everything and that they are not able to handle things on their own. They have the humility to own up to their mistakes and accept advice from others. Sharing credit and allowing others to take the initiative are other traits of a modest leader. And last, a humble leader is receptive to criticism and flexible in their thinking when needed.

What Traits And Attributes Distinguish Successful Leaders?

1. Interaction One of the most important competencies in a
 toolbox is good communication. Great leaders use this ability to communicate concepts, ideas, and plans while also creating a sense of unity and purpose among the team members. The most engaged staff members will be able to tell a leader's authenticity level by their tone of voice, thus how they say something can often be just as significant as what they say. It can be quite successful to combine the leadership trait of empathy with an emphasis on better communication. A leader's team is more likely to pay attention and obey when their actions show that they have listened to and considered what others have said.

2. Making decisions: Your organization's executive team makes all the final decisions. Leaders are the ones who have to evaluate all the information available to them and make a decision, regardless of whether they are in charge of a group of five people or are seated in the C-suite.

3. Assigning Delegating tasks and duties to other staff members is a challenge for many bosses: This is especially true for leaders moving up the leadership ladder, such as when a sales director becomes the CRO and has to start thinking about the organization's priorities instead of simply the sales department. On the other hand, effective task delegation is essential to the smooth running of leadership teams and the entire company. That serves the organization's best interests. Being human, all leaders may occasionally experience "deer in the headlights" moments when the weight of making a choice feels too great. Leaders who practice mindfulness will be better able to handle these challenging decisions. Simply observe when fear creeps in, accept it, and let your principles guide you.

4. Self-knowledge: Everyone in an organization can benefit from reflecting on their own strengths and flaws. A strong leader is aware of their feelings and can recognize their own prejudices and how they could affect the way they lead. Leaders who possess the ability to objectively examine themselves are capable of understanding how others feel and act because they can put themselves in their shoes. Because of this, self-awareness is a crucial leadership trait that contributes to emotional intelligence.

5. Quickness: Being agile as an organization is not a destination. It's an ongoing process of learning new things, getting better, and making adjustments as needed. Felix Hieronymus, the corporate project leader of Bosch, stated in a Forbes insights study that "you cannot become agile without changing your behavior and your mindset." It isn't about turning the business around and then declaring triumph or success. The goal is to get the business to the point where it continuously learns and adjusts. His observation emphases that agility should be ingrained in an organization's culture rather than something that can be quantified.

SECTION FIVE

What Is Business Financing

The term "business financing" describes the range of methods by which companies can raise the capital required to launch, maintain, and grow their activities. Business finance comes in a variety of forms, such as crowdfunding, venture capital, and bank loans. Let's examine each of these choices in more detail.

One of the most popular ways to finance a business is through bank loans. Any amount of money borrowed from a bank with interest-bearing repayment terms is called a bank loan. Usually, in order to secure the loan, the bank will need collateral, such as a home or other assets.

Another popular source of funding for businesses is venture capital. Professional investors, such as venture capitalists or angel investors, provide money to a firm in exchange for an equity stake. This is known as venture capital. These investors frequently anticipate receiving a large return on their capital, and they might also offer the business counsel and direction.

A relatively new method of financing businesses, crowdfunding is collecting money from many people, typically via an internet platform. Money contributed to a crowdsourcing campaign is usually given to the firm in support or in exchange for a good or service.

Debt Financing: What Is It? Debt funding for your company Any money borrowed from a lender, such as banks, credit unions, or other financial institutions, is referred to as debt financing. When using debt financing, the business owner has a predetermined amount of time to return the loan plus interest. Debt finance offers a number of benefits. It is typically simpler to secure than equity financing and permits the business owner to maintain control over the enterprise.

Debt financing, however, carries a higher risk of cost in the event that the company is unable to repay the loan.

Equity financing is an additional choice. Money raised through the sale of ownership shares in the company to investors is known as equity financing. One benefit of equity financing is that it can provide cash without requiring loan repayment. It also entails ceding some managerial authority over the business, and the owner could have to split earnings with investors. Additionally, it could be more challenging to locate investors ready to finance a new or small business with equity.

Business Financing Types

There are numerous varieties of finance available for businesses, such as:

- Term loans: Term loans are large sums of money with fixed interest rates that are repaid over a predetermined length of time.

- Credit lines: A credit line offers access to a predetermined sum of money that can be accessed as needed, much like a credit card. Only interest is paid by the business owner on borrowed funds.

 - Merchant cash advances: These are a form of short-term loan that are repaid using a portion of the company's credit card sales.

- Crowdfunding: Usually conducted via internet platforms, crowdfunded are a means to collect money from a sizable number of individuals.

Peer-to-peer lending: Peer-to-peer lending is a lending model where lenders and borrowers are connected to one other.

- Venture capital: Financing supplied by venture capitalists, who are usually seasoned investors, is known as venture capital. Apart from these two typical funding solutions, there are more options as well.

- Invoice factoring: By selling their outstanding bills to a factoring company, businesses can use invoice factoring to acquire cash fast. After that, the factoring company gets the money from the client.

- Microloans: Usually provided by nonprofit or community-based organizations, microloans are little loans. They are frequently employed to support new enterprises or companies located in low-income areas.

- Business funding: The government or other organizations may be able to provide funds to certain enterprises. There are many kinds of lenders in addition to the different kinds of company finance.

- Banks: The most popular source of funding for businesses is a bank. Typically, they provide a range of credit cards and loans.

- Credit unions: Credit unions are membership-owned financial organizations. Compared to banks, they frequently provide cheaper interest rates.

- Online lenders: A more recent choice, online lenders provide rapid and simple funding access. Their interest rates could be greater than those of other lenders, nevertheless. It's also critical to comprehend the many terminologies utilized in the financing of businesses.

Typical Terms Include The Following:

- Collateral: An asset used to guarantee a loan is known as collateral. The collateral may be seized by the lender to cover their losses in the event that the business owner fails on the loan.

- Loan term: The time frame within which the loan must be returned is known as the loan term.

- APR: The cost of the loan, including interest and any other costs, is expressed as the annual percentage rate, or APR. -

SBA loans: The Small Business Administration insures these types of loans.

Benefits of Debt Accrual Using Debt To Finance Your Business Has A Number Of Benefits:

1. The lending institution does not own your business; it has no say over how you operate it.

2. Your relationship with the lender terminates when you repay the debt. As the value of your business increases, that becomes even more crucial.

3. You can deduct interest paid on debt financing from your taxes as a business expense.

4. You can incorporate the monthly payment and its breakdown in your forecasting models with accuracy because they are known expenses

SECTION SIX

Inventory Management

The process of controlling the movement of items into and out of a business is known as inventory management. This entails maintaining tabs on the inventory that is currently in stock, as well as what needs to be ordered, when and in what quantity. Businesses can minimize expenses and prevent stock-outs by practicing good inventory management. Inventory management can be done in a number of ways, such as material needs planning (MRP), just-in-time inventory, and economic order quantity (EOQ). The ideal approach for a given firm will vary depending on its size, nature, and goods sold.

An essential component of corporate financing is inventory management. Efficient inventory management can lower expenses and increase cash flow. Real-time inventory level tracking is one of the best techniques for inventory management.
- Determining the reorder points so that stock is topped off before it runs out.

Utilizing software for inventory management to optimize the procedure.
- Monitoring inventory expenditures to ascertain profitability.
- Reducing the quantity of inventory retained by putting just-in-time inventory management into practice.
These tactics can help companies increase their cash flow and maintain low inventory expenses.

Motives Behind Maintaining Inventory

1. Accommodate changes in production demand
The production plan is adjusted based on orders, stocking patterns, projections, and sales. Because of this, the requirement for raw material supply for production fluctuates depending on the product strategy, including batch amounts and individual SKUs.

Keeping supplies at a close-by warehouse makes it easier to send the right amount and item to production on schedule.

2. Meet Seasonal and Cyclical Needs

Seasons, holidays, and other factors affect market demand and supply, and historical sales data enables businesses to predict significant spikes in demand well in advance. As a result, they hoard inventory and stockpile raw resources in order to boost production and quickly bring more products to market in order to satisfy the rising demand.

3. Scale Economies in Procurement

The cost to the business of purchasing raw materials in greater amounts and keeping inventory is shown to be lower than purchasing small lots often. In these situations, one makes bulk purchases and keeps inventory at the plant warehouse.

4. Benefit from Quantity Discounts and Price Increases

In anticipation of future price increases stemming from factors such as shifting supply and demand in domestic or global markets, tax implications, budgetary constraints, etc., companies typically purchase raw materials ahead of time and maintain inventory to protect themselves from rising expenses.

Purchasing in bulk and keeping raw material inventories is how businesses take advantage of the supplier's quantity discounts. In these circumstances, the savings from the discount would be far more than the cost of carrying the inventory.

5. Cut Down on Transit Time and Cost
Purchasing raw materials in bulk and shipping them as a complete truck load or container load might result in significant transportation cost savings whether importing raw materials from overseas or from a remote source within the nation. Part shipments may be more expensive.

The transit time for a full truck load or container shipment is also quicker and more direct than for a partial shipment load, which may require several weeks as the goods forwarder waits for more loads to fill the container.

Numerous causes may contribute to transportation delays and shipping delays, which can disrupt the supply chain and force businesses to keep raw material inventories on hand as a safety measure.

6. Items with a long lead time and high demand must be kept in stock.
Raw material suppliers can have lengthy lead times of many months. In addition, one should anticipate supply disruptions if the specific item is in high demand and low supply. Control and inventory holding are safer in these situations.

The Price Of Maintaining Inventory

There Are Three Primary Types Of Inventory Costs:

1.opportunity costs

2.carrying costs

3.storage costs.

The expenses related to managing and keeping inventory,
including

1.capital costs

2.Insurance

3.taxes

Are known as carrying costs. The expenses of the physical space required to hold inventory, such as utilities and rent, are referred to as storage costs. Opportunity costs are the expenses incurred when funds intended for inventory are not used for other endeavors, including investments or corporate growth. All these expenses should be taken into account by businesses when deciding how much inventory to keep on hand.

Let's examine carrying expenses in more detail. These are the continuous expenses associated with keeping inventory, and they might change according on the kind of goods, where it is kept, and how long it is kept. The cost of capital, taxes, and insurance make up the bulk of carrying expenses. The premiums paid to cover goods against loss or damage are known as insurance expenses. Sales tax, property tax, inventory tax, and other taxes are examples of the taxes that need to be paid on inventory.

Let's examine the cost of capital next. This is the amount of money spent on inventory purchases.

The computation involves multiplying the interest rate of the loan utilized to fund the inventory by the total amount borrowed. For instance, the cost of capital for a business borrowing $10,000 at a 5% interest rate would be $500. When assessing the inventory's profitability, this expense needs to be taken into account. The company may be losing money by keeping such inventory if the cost of capital exceeds the benefit from it.

Storing merchandise comes with additional expenses, such as spoiling and shrinking. The loss of inventory as a result of spoiling, expiration, or obsolescence is known as spoilage. Inventory loss as a result of theft, damage, or mistake is known as shrinkage. When deciding what to stock, these expenses should be taken into account. They can be calculated using industry averages and historical data. Lastly, to guarantee that inventory is maintained effectively and that expenses are kept to a minimum, it should be routinely checked.

CHAPTER SEVEN

Cultural Quirks And How They Affect Marketing

Tactics marketers are aware of how closely advertising and culture are related; both influence and reflect societal norms on attitudes, values, and behavior. Advertising is a potent force for cultural innovation and change, even as it mirrors societal conventions and trends.

The Share a Coke campaign by Coca-Cola, for instance, is a great illustration of how advertising can empower societal change. Coca-Cola replaced the iconic names from several cultures on the bottles for this promotion. The goal of the campaign was to get consumers to share Coke and view the beverage as a personalized gift. The brand made use of the social significance of drinking with friends and family and connected it to the cultural significance of names.

The audience's perception is shaped by culture, which affects how they understand and remember advertisements. Ads that are tailored to the target market's and society's cultural norms and expectations have a higher chance of being remembered and doing well than those that don't pay attention to them.

But does it actually affect how memorable an advertisement is? And how can brands use culture to their advantage to make memorable advertisements? We shall examine the subtleties of how various facets of culture affect the memorability of the advertisement in order to comprehend this.

Cultural Aspects and How They Affect the Memorability of the Ad

Among the cultural elements that have a direct bearing on how memorable an advertisement is are language, values, habits, rituals, behaviors, and beliefs. These parameters vary throughout cultural contexts. Therefore, it is crucial to keep them in mind when focusing on your target demographic and creating messages and campaigns if you want your commercials to stick in their memory.

1. Language: Your audience and you communicate primarily through language, thus the words you use will have a direct influence on how well your advertisement is received, comprehended, and remembered. It is essentially a cultural object that subtly—and sometimes not so subtly—reflects trends and conventions.

It grows and changes in response to the culture; for example, slang, phrases, expressions, meanings, and implications emerge to represent the prevailing attitudes and tendencies of a certain era.

2. Values: Culture, or our environment, defines normative behavior, or what is desirable and acceptable behavior. It also assigns positions to people within the social structure and establishes values and tenets for our daily life. These principles, which help us distinguish between what is good and harmful, are ingrained in us. Diverse cultures also have quite different values. For instance, in eastern or Indian cultures, collectivism is valued more highly than individuality, whereas in western or American cultures, the opposite is true.

3. Customs and Rituals: In China, calligraphy is very popular; in India, henna tattoos are popular during weddings and festivals; and in western

nations, Christmas is very popular. These traditions and rites are defined by culture, and people from different cultures usually take them very seriously. These traditions and practices typically set limits or rules for what can and cannot be used in advertisements. While it is acceptable to cross some lines in order to convey messages of respect, inclusivity, and other positive things, most of the audience may find this uncomfortable or non resonant because customs are very significant in cultural groups, particularly those that prioritize religion. Thus, there is a fine line that advertisers must tread to reconcile their brand's reputation with creating an unforgettable advertisement.

4. Practices/Norms: Cultural norms and practices have a big influence on how we conduct our daily lives. These include the language we speak, the clothes we wear, the food we consume, the holidays we observe, and the social interactions we partake in. Advertisements that faithfully depict these customs and standards strike a deep chord with viewers. These advertisements elicit a favorable emotional response that helps the viewer register the ad and the brand favorably, which directly affects the ad's memorability.

Social Media's Function In International Product Launches

Global product introductions are greatly influenced by social media. It can be used to engage with potential customers, build excitement and buzz around new products, and encourage word-of-mouth marketing. Utilizing social media sites like Facebook, Instagram, and Twitter makes it simple and quick to reach a big audience. Social media is another tool that brands can use to interact with customers and build a community around their goods. Social media has even occasionally been used to crowdsource features and ideas for new products.

Apple's release of the iPhone X is a prime example. Before the product was released, the corporation teased it on social media sites like Twitter and Instagram to create buzz and anticipation. Following the product's launch, Apple kept up its social media promotion and customer service on these platforms. The iPhone X became one of the most well-liked cellphones ever after its launch, which was met with great success.

SECTION EIGHT

Digital Transformation's Effect On Company Sales

Digital transformation has significantly changed how companies market and sell their goods and services. Businesses used to mostly rely on conventional marketing strategies like print advertisements and billboards. However, since social media and the internet have grown in popularity, businesses now need to adjust to a new environment. To reach their target audience, they must have a strong online presence and employ digital strategies like social media ads, SEO, and email marketing. This transition has been most noticeable in the retail sector, where e-commerce has fundamentally altered how companies market their goods.

The development of omnichannel retailing has been one of the main effects of the digital revolution. Using a range of offline and online platforms, firms employ this method to reach their target audience. A retailer, for instance, might have physical storefronts, a smartphone app, and a website. Regardless of the shopping method a consumer chooses, the aim is to provide a smooth experience for them. Businesses can now reach a wider audience and sell more goods thanks to this, which has completely changed the game for them.

Personalisation has become more popular as a result of digital transformation. This is the process of customizing the buying encounter for every single consumer. For instance, a merchant may recommend products based on a customer's past purchases and browsing activities. Personalized emails or push notifications may also be sent according to the interests of a customer. A more relevant and meaningful experience for the customer is the aim of personalisation, and this eventually results in increased sales.

The rise of data-driven decision making is the last effect of the digital transformation. This is the process of using analytics and data to guide business choices, such as those made on marketing initiatives and product development. Businesses used to mostly rely on experience and intuition when making choices. However, as big data has grown in popularity, people may now use real-time data to make better decisions. As a result, business decision-making now takes a more scientific approach, which benefits companies by increasing productivity and profitability. Personalisation is essential for corporate marketing. Using data to target and retarget leads with a brand message that directly addresses their interests, demographics, and purchasing patterns is known as marketing personalisation. Your customers should believe that the brand message was created specifically for them when you use a personalized marketing plan. Thus, individual or one-to-one marketing are other terms for personalized marketing.

Businesses such as Netflix, Amazon, and YouTube strategically employ personalisation by utilizing an algorithm to automatically propose items, series, and videos for your perusal.
These suggestions are derived from information gathered from the things you look for, buy, and watch, as well as from the watching preferences of other people who share your interests. Customer interaction is simply one advantage of personalisation; it's not limited to digital media. If patrons see that they are receiving a customized and tailored experience, they are more inclined to return to their preferred lodging establishments, coffee shops, or salons. When a brand makes them feel special.

1.Improved relationship with clients. For example, your email is more likely to convert if it contains personalized elements such as the names of your leads and other relevant information. Furthermore, according to 73% of consumers, they prefer doing business with companies who customize their emails.

2. Increased earnings. Customers are more likely to make repeat purchases when they have a personalized shopping experience, and brands that offer these services see an increase in transactional rates, buyer retention, and revenue per transaction.

3. Better targeting of buyers. When is the ideal moment to communicate with your clients? How much interaction do they desire? Understanding your audience is a crucial component of personalisation, since customers appreciate it when brands know when and how to approach them while maintaining a polite conversation.

4. A more robust brand image. Customers purchase products from brands that offer them a positive customer experience. Consider a name like Chewy, a pet supply firm. They will personally get in touch to offer condolences if they learn that a

customer has stopped placing orders due to the death of their pet. Personal experiences like these leave a deep impression and help a business gain the loyalty of its clients over time.

5. Improved consumer remarketing and lead creation. Resolving issues that your target audience faces fosters trust and increases the likelihood that they will send you feedback and information.

How Can You Go Beyond The Obstacles In Branding?

1. Defining your brand: Establishing your brand is one of the first and most important phases in brand marketing. Clarifying your goals, values, tone, style, personality, and mission is necessary to achieve this. You will struggle to convey your message, draw in your target market, and set yourself apart from competitors without a precise and consistent brand definition. In order to overcome this obstacle, you must carry out an exhaustive brand audit, investigate your industry and rivals, and develop a brand strategy that complements your objectives and target audience.

2. Producing captivating material: Developing captivating content that highlights your company's benefits and establishes a connection with your audience is another frequent problem in brand marketing. Whether it's a blog post, video, podcast, or social media post, content is what powers your brand marketing campaigns. But producing material that is timely, worthwhile, and reliable may be difficult, expensive, and time-consuming. You must organize your content strategy, make use of the appropriate platforms and tools, and track the effectiveness of your material if you want to overcome this obstacle.

3. Upholding brand consistency: Establishing a robust and identifiable brand identity requires upholding brand consistency. Making sure that all of your channels and touchpoints use your logo, colors, fonts, pictures, and voice consistently is known as brand consistency. But it can be difficult to keep your brand consistent, particularly if you have several teams, partners, or agencies involved in your brand marketing. To overcome this obstacle.

SECTION NINE

Impact Of Sale: Direct Versus Indirect Methods Of Distribution

A business that sells directly to customers organizes and manages the distribution route known as "direct distribution." In this scenario, the business handles every facet of delivery internally (as opposed to relying on outside parties) and bears complete accountability for guaranteeing that clients receive their orders satisfactorily. Setting up direct channels can be more expensive and involve more work. In actuality, they might need a substantial capital outlay. It is necessary to set up trucks, delivery personnel, warehouses, and logistical systems. The direct channel will probably be shorter, less complicated, and less expensive than an indirect channel after that is finished.

A distribution route known as "indirect distribution" uses middlemen to carry out the distribution tasks for a business. By releasing the manufacturer from some of the initial obligations and costs associated with direct distribution, it can free up more time for business operations.

In addition, an indirect distribution route can be far easier to operate than a direct distribution channel with the correct vendor relationships. It can provide much-needed help and distribution knowledge that a business might not have.

Benefits Of Direct Distribution Routes

Direct distribution channels are advantageous to both customers and businesses in a number of ways. Companies can swiftly increase their earnings and set themselves apart from rivals by using this kind of distribution. The following are the primary benefits of direct channels:

1. Total control over the supply chain: Businesses can handle all of their own shipping and transactional processes when they use direct routes of distribution. This implies that they won't have to rely on a middleman and can maintain control over the level of service. Businesses that

control and maintain their product supply may guarantee excellent customer support.

2. Ownership of supply chain assets: Companies using this model are the owners of the transportation, logistics, and warehousing facilities needed to fulfil client orders. This guarantees that a business is not dependent on wholesalers and can reliably complete consumer orders. The business gains benefit from owning these assets as well.

3. Increased sales revenue: A direct distribution approach avoids middlemen who purchase goods at a discount and resell them for a profit. Producers in this case do not get paid the full amount for the product from the customer. Because they don't split their profits with distributors, wholesalers, and retailers, businesses that employ direct methods of distribution keep a larger portion of their earnings.

4. Direct input: By providing their clients with direct service, businesses can get feedback. Sending out surveys is one method of getting input. Companies can then apply the input to enhance consumer satisfaction and product quality, which can lead to a rise in recurring business.

5. Put an emphasis on quality: Companies that use direct distribution channels can establish and uphold standards for quality throughout their entire organization. They are able to design and execute the most efficient processes for product production, marketing, packaging, and delivery. This guarantees constant order fulfillment and high-quality products.

The Drawbacks Of Using Direct Distribution Channels

Not every business is a good fit for direct methods of distribution. Businesses should weigh the benefits and drawbacks of using this strategy for product sales. The primary drawbacks are as follows:

1. High initial costs: Businesses must pay for the storage and transportation of goods when using this kind of distribution. Postage costs, fleet car operations, and warehouse ownership or leasing can soon add up and cut into revenues. These expenses are typically covered by the middlemen who sell the goods.

2. Added workload: A company that takes on full supply chain management gains extra responsibilities such as product marketing and sales as well as order fulfillment from customers. For companies who used indirect distribution in the past, this can be a significant shift.

3. Too much to focus on: Direct product production and sales expose businesses to a larger range of activities. They may have too much to concentrate on as a result. There may be less focus on developing the best product if the practical processes of processing customer orders, inquiries, and complaints are managed instead of the order fulfillment process.

How To Include The Four Ps In Your Marketing Strategy

The four Ps are the essential factors that need to be carefully examined and properly applied in order to effectively sell a good or service. Product, pricing, location, and promotion are them.

The Four Ps of Marketing Are These

1. Product: Understanding the product is the first step in developing a marketing strategy. Why and who needs it? What does it do that no product from a competitor can match? Maybe it's something completely different and when customers see it, they won't be able to resist buying it due to its attractive appearance or functionality.

2. Price: The price of a product is the amount that buyers are willing to pay. Marketing professionals need to take into account supply costs, seasonal discounts, retail markup, rivals' prices, and the product's perceived and actual worth when determining the price of the product.

Business decision-makers occasionally decide to increase a product's price to make it appear more exclusive or luxurious. Or, they might reduce the cost to entice more customers to give it a try.

3. Place: Place refers to the product's intended retail location, including both physical and virtual storefronts, as well as the way it will be exhibited.

A luxury cosmetic product manufacturer would prefer to have their product exhibited in Sephora and Neiman Marcus rather than in Walmart or

Family Dollar. This is a crucial decision. Getting their items in front of the customers who are most inclined to purchase them is the constant objective of business executives.

4. Promotion: The purpose of promotion is to inform the public that this product is necessary and that its pricing is reasonable. Public relations, advertising, and the entire media plan for a product's introduction are all included in promotion.

SECTION TEN

How Does Product Placement Affect Consumer Purchase Decisions?

Product Placement: What Is It?

A production that is intended for a broad audience may incorporate branded products and services as part of a product placement campaign. Product placements, also referred to as "embedded marketing" or "embedded advertising," are frequently seen in motion pictures, TV shows, home videos, radio, and—less frequently—live performances. Companies may pay a production company or studio in cash, commodities, or services in exchange for the right to use a studio's work in product placement.

How Is Product Placement Operational?

Product placements are used, mentioned, or discussed throughout the programme in a way that will elicit favorable feelings towards the promoted brand. They're not pornographic ads. Product placement works because, as opposed to being advertised directly, it helps the audience form a deeper bond with the brand in a more organic way. It is most usually the result of an advertiser's payment for that right when a brand appears in a film, television programme, or other performance. Some individuals think that this kind of advertising is inherently dishonest and misleading to impressionable youngsters.

What Effect Do These Have On Purchasing Decisions?

How consumers purchase goods can be significantly impacted by product placement. For instance, studies have indicated that products arranged on shelves at eye level had a higher purchase probability than those positioned lower.

Aisle product placement is another illustration. Products positioned near points of heavy circulation, such as aisle ends, have a higher chance of being noticed and bought than those positioned farther away. Businesses can utilize this to their advantage when determining how best to distribute their goods. Businesses can utilize data to determine where to put products based on their understanding of how customers navigate stores. Businesses can utilize this information, for instance, to position confectionery and other impulsive buys close to checkout lanes. By utilizing the way customers navigate the store, this can boost sales.

Going a step further, let's discuss how businesses may leverage big data to optimize their supply chains. The mechanism that transports goods from the producer to the consumer is known as the supply chain. This covers every aspect, including transportation and inventory control. Through supply chain data analysis, businesses may optimize operations and cut expenses. It's a really strong tool! Let's now discuss a few concrete instances of big data being applied by businesses to supply chain optimisation. One excellent example is Amazon. To optimize their supply chain, they have made significant investments in machine learning and data analytics. They have been able to cut expenses and increase productivity as a result. Walmart is yet another illustration. They alter their layout and product placement based on data they collect to understand how people navigate their stores.

Colors' Impact On Consumer Decision-Making

There exists a potent psychological impact of colors and a strong correlation between color and emotions. Because color has the power to arouse emotions, it also has the ability to alter our behavior. For example, a red sports vehicle can arouse feelings of excitement, while a blue sea can calm us down. Science backs this up as well because color satisfies a basic neurological demand for stimulation. The brain and the body as a whole respond to color in very particular ways. For example, blue lowers heart rate, blood pressure, and respiration rate while red increases heart rate and blood pressure. For marketers, color can be crucial to a company's identity as well as a means of differentiating the brand and implying emotional benefits. It has a strong psychological impact. Furthermore, it goes beyond the product's color. Purchase selections may also be influenced by the color of the store. For instance, research indicates that customers are more likely to spend money in stores that have cool colors like blue and green.

So How Does It Affect How Consumers Make Decisions?

1. Colour and Marketing: It's important to remember that consumers prioritize color and visual appearance over other aspects when making purchases (96 percent visual appearance, 6% texture, and 1% sound or scent).

85% of consumers cite color as the main factor in their decision to purchase a certain item.
Shades and Logos
Brand identification rises by 80% when color is used. Customer confidence is directly correlated with brand recognition.

2. Colour and the Consumer: One of the most effective design techniques is color. It is not, however, completely universal (the colors that

arouse interest in India differ from those in North America).

3.Overall Design: A lot of online customers attribute their decision to not make a purchase from a certain website (42%) and not visit it again (52%), to poor overall design and website navigability.

4.Time: Among the several reasons why customers are visiting online stores again are speed, efficiency, and convenience. A website that loads even five seconds slower than your rivals' could cost you a lot of money—64 percent of online buyers will not complete a purchase because of a slow-loading website.

5. Power words: Retailers depend on words' capacity to arouse feelings in their audience. Selecting the appropriate "power" term could be the difference between a customer choosing to buy the same product at one retail location over another.

When a sales sign is displayed in the window, 52% of customers are more inclined to enter the store. 60% of customers are more at ease and inclined to purchase a product that has the phrase "guaranteed" attached to it.

How Marketing Narratives Influence Consumers' Perceptions

Telling stories has benefits beyond merely endorsing goods or services. It involves creating a brand atmosphere that captivates consumers, arouses their emotions, and motivates them to act.

However, it goes beyond that. It all comes down to creating an experience that your audience won't soon forget and that forges much deeper connections. Using narratives, marketers are able to create a stronger and more engaging emotional connection with consumers than they can with more conventional incentives like cost, perks, or loyalty schemes.

www.ingramcontent.com/pod-product-compliance
Lightning Source LLC
Chambersburg PA
CBHW062246290526
45794CB00006B/2432